SEXUAL ABUSE

Jacques Louis David

Gotham Books

30 N Gould St.
Ste. 20820, Sheridan, WY 82801
https://gothambooksinc.com/

Phone: 1 (307) 464-7800

© 2024 *Jacques Louis David*. All rights reserved.

No part of this book may be reproduced, stored in a retrieval system, or transmitted by any means without the written permission of the author.

Published by Gotham Books (August 20, 2024)

ISBN: 979-8-3303-0378-6 (H)
ISBN: 979-8-88775-986-9 (P)
ISBN: 979-8-88775-987-6 (E)

Because of the dynamic nature of the Internet, any web addresses or links contained in this book may have changed since publication and may no longer be valid.

The views expressed in this work are solely those of the author and do not necessarily reflect the views of the publisher, and the publisher hereby disclaims any responsibility for them.

My name is Jacques Louis David,

I was born on January 14th, 1966, at 12:41 a.m.
I can't remember the hospital.

Now, this is all hearsay.

I don't remember much of my childhood living with my mother and father.

They often told me about my first few years.

I was born what is called a blue baby,

The cord was wrapped around my neck when I came out.

I was put into an incubator and was in there for forty minutes with aided breathing,

I am told it was forty minutes before I could breathe on my own.

I don't know how true it is.

I'm just telling you what I was told.

I am also told that my mother drank several bottles of wine.

A month and smoked several packs of cigarettes a month throughout,

Her whole pregnancy was in 1966, so I guess it was okay then.

I am lucky I didn't come out an FAS baby.

One thing is for certain: my entire life...

It is riddled with the sickness of one kind or another person that can be blamed on that.

First of all, congenital hypertension, which is born with high blood pressure, is very rare.

I don't know when, but as an infant, I had a hernia surgery.

It was later attributed to a condition that was,

I can't remember what it was called,

A hardening of a section of my intestines.

So, there was also surgery on my stomach.

All the way across from one side of the other, a couple of inches underneath my belly button.

To cut out that piece of intestine and then reattach the two okay sections of my intestine,

I can imagine it was very difficult because I was so small,

But that happened a second time.

I imagine it was only a few inches long when I was an infant, but now it's thirteen or fourteen inches,

It grew as I grew, very strange.

Daly City was a two-year venture.

My father supported us by diving for abalone.

I know, crazy, huh? I was told he was so good.

He could stay underwater for eight minutes.

He farmed enough abalone to support a wife and a son for 2 years in Daly City.

I remember getting my diaper changed,

I remember getting cleaned,

I also remember my mother sucking my dick.

I did not get hard.

I did not feel anything; at the time, I did not know it was wrong. It was just part of life.

It happened a few more times.

I don't know why, but we moved to La Habra, California, after a while.

I remember the apartment,

I remember the Jehovah's Witness Kingdom Hall across from our apartment complex,

And I remember the two extremely abusive Mexican twins who were our babysitters.

They used to tie me to a post in the garage and throw lawn darts at me. Very painful.

I have a very vivid memory of a cliff that the apartments were underneath,

Perhaps twenty or thirty feet tall. Maybe an eighty-degree slant.

I remember dragging my bicycle by its rear tire up that cliff and finally riding my bike down.

That cliff into the driveway of our apartments,

I almost got run over by my father as he drove in.

I got in trouble for that. I also vividly remember having a slingshot with metal steel balls.

I remember going through it in my mind.

I would get into a lot of trouble, but it would be worth it.

I think you might know where this is going.

We had a fish tank. Based on fifty-seven years of experience.

I'm guessing it was a freshwater fish tank because the fish were gold.

I shot it with the slingshot and then ran to my room.

It did break, but they never came to me.

It didn't occur to them that I did it, I guess.

I feel bad now because all the fish died.

At that point in time, I didn't understand that, so I didn't feel bad for that.

But yes, I did feel bad for breaking the fish tank.

I remember the twins throwing my sister's tricycle in the air, and when it landed, it broke,

I remember she screamed to my parents.

But she couldn't tell them the truth, and I got in trouble.

It wasn't pretty.

I got beat pretty bad.,

One of my favorite things for my mother to do was to shout at us to get over here,

I'm going to slap your face,

She'd hit me so hard.

I would fall on the floor or fly across the room and slam into the wall.

It was more me than my sister.

I am told when we lived in that apartment complex,

That, my mother, fed me coriander leaves from the coriander trees that were lining our apartment complex,

Which led to my being hospitalized and my stomach being pumped.

Also, when I was a baby.

I'm told she threw me at a wall because I would not stop crying.

As I dictate this...

It occurs to me that I'm surprised I'm alive right now.

During these couple of years, I've not been very healthy.

I remember a lot of time in the hospital.

I remember a woman with a white hat on.

All dressed in white with the gigantic needle, of course,

I'm a baby, so it's gigantic.

I don't remember the pain of it.

There was a great deal of medication if my memory serves me correctly,

It was 127 pills three times a day.

At one point in time,

I started hiding the pills. Of course, I got caught.

My mother blended all of the pills with dehydrated milk and water.

She would lay me flat on the floor and trap me with her knees over my arms.

Then, force-feed me the concoction with a turkey baster.

As I think about it,

I'm surprised that I didn't throw it all up because it tasted like vomit.

I remember hanging out with the Pike family.

Toby Pike. Debbie Pike and several more.

We all went hopping one day at a farmer's market or something like that with all the kids hanging out,

I didn't know too much about food...

So, when Toby dared me to eat a long yellow thing.

I didn't even hesitate,

I was hospitalized with blisters in my mouth.

Even now, I would rather taste my food than feel it.

There is such a thing as too.

Yes, you guessed it. It was a pepper.

I don't know what kind but it was very hot.

It took a couple of decades before I could start doing hot stuff again.

The sexual abuse changed a little bit.

My mother taught me how to use my little arm as a kind of dildo.

She always smelled so bad.

I wasn't privy to the conversations,

That my parents and my doctors had.

I wasn't in the same room.

My parents did finally say that they saw smog in Los Angeles had a bad effect on me, and we had to move to a fresher air.

We moved to Tehachapi.

My uncle, my sister's brother,

And also, the elder of the Jehovah's Witness congregation let us with him and his family for a few months.

Two daughters, wife, husband, and my father, mother, and sister.

It was a little crowded.

The sexual abuse was compounded by physical abuse.

Do you remember those two-foot by? I think 6 feet wall heaters.

They had a pilot light that you had to get down on the ground, push some buttons, and hold for sixty seconds before the pilot light was hit. Then, you would hear this wash of flame.

Then your house would suddenly start getting warmer.

My uncle would put a paddle.

Then I would get in trouble for something, and I had to try to get that paddle off the top of that heater.

Sometimes, I would burn myself on the. The longer it took.

The more he would hit me with it when I finally got it, the more the rest of the family would hit me.

I would be watching and laughing as I tried to get that pedal down as fast as possible.

I don't know when he started, but sometimes,

He found a time when he could take me privately into his room.

Tie my hands behind my back.

Tie my feet together, then tie those two things together.

hogtie basically, ...

with another person in the room that I can't remember,

Then they would pick me up like a suitcase and force me to suck my uncle's dick.

My mother and my uncle were both obese, and he smelled just like her.

I remember shoulder pain.

Fortunately, he didn't cum in my mouth, but instead,

He came in a plastic bag.

I don't know if it was a Ziploc, but it was something like that.

He would write my name, the date, and the hour and then tie it up with a metal bendy tie-up.

He had a chest full of them.

As I think about it, that kind of tells me...

He's been doing it for a while with others.

It happened a few more times.

I am guessing it only took a few more months.

But my parents found a house, and we literally moved to the wrong side of the tracks. I remember playing with kids.

I remember a babysitter that I used to give oral sex to,

Remember, I'm still a kid, so I don't know if that's wrong.

Again, I don't remember exactly, but I think we were there for three or four more years,

And then we moved to a better house.

Still living on the wrong side of the tracks but a better house.

I remember a three-speed bicycle and getting pretty good at riding it,

One day, I remember riding it with no hands.

I didn't know what it meant but was flipping off the world.

I remember hitting a sandy section and going down.

Man, that was bad. The strawberries were on my legs, on my stomach, on my arms, and on my face.

I must clarify,

All I was wearing was shorts, no shoes,

No, anything, just shorts. I tried to hide it.

I think I was successful.

Nobody ever asked me what happened.

I do remember, around seven years old, talking my sister into sex.

I didn't know what it meant, but my neighbor was there, and we all pretended to have sex, or at least I pretended.

I later apologize to her.

I remember getting really good grades. Straight A's even,

My parents sat me down at the kitchen table.

One night, when they brought the report card home and told me not to try so hard in school,

That the world was going to end in a few years.

I didn't listen.

But they sat me down many times with the same information.

I used to have fruit wars with the kids across the street.

We would throw peaches. They would throw oranges.

Kevin Butrerbret, Good times! I remember a cat had some kittens underneath our house.

My dad got them out.

He handed one to me, and I dropped her off, but it turned out okay.

We found homes for all the kittens. And we kept two.

I love cats...

I was, I think, seven when my parents divorced when we lived in this house.

Maybe eight or so?

I remember he lived a couple of houses down for a while.

We went there for a visit.

It didn't seem strange to me then.

He made some amazing chili for us that night.

I wish I knew how he made it.

My mother worked for an assemblyman.

She cleaned his house every day.

He owned a dilapidated duplex that we ended up moving into.

One side of the front room was my bedroom.

My bed was pushed up against the front door with several broken windows.

During winter, snow would come in through.

Those broken planes fall on my head.

I loved it...

My sister's bedroom was on the other side, and my mother slept in the front room.

She often slept naked...

The sexual abuse turned into physical abuse.

She would make me get a switch from off a tree in the front yard,

And beat me with it, or she slapped me in the face so hard.

I would fly across the room.

She hit me in the kidney once with the table leg.

I used to sneak out and explore the town.

So, amazing those memories,

I hated the abuse, but I loved I had chronological alone time.

There is so much going through my mind right now,

I'll keep as much as I can chronological, but there will be a little craziness.

I remember a giant pine tree in the backyard.

Somewhere in time,

I saw a man's climate tree with spikes in his boots and rope loosely wrapped around the tree.

I was able to do the same.

I would climb that tree every day.

Now, remember, I still did not have anything to compare in life,

The abuse, sexual or otherwise, was just part of life to me.

So, in my mind, life was pretty good at that time.

I remember all the families getting together, and a summer camping in the Tehachapi mountains for a week or two.

I remember one night, my mother made spaghetti with sauce.

I had ten very big oval plates.

It was a good night for me.

Nobody stopped me.

I also remember losing control running down a meadow in the mountains.

I almost fell several times.

After the divorce,

I remember making it to the town dump.

I don't remember who it was with,

But the rich kids that lived in Bear Valley Springs,

I would throw away some really good stuff,

One year, we got a couple of brand-new bicycles, more than two.

I would cannibalize all these bikes and make a supercross bike.

Perhaps a couple of times over.

I would bring that bike to me with school and sell it for fifty or sixty bucks.

Back in the day.

That was quite a bit. In elementary school, we had a pseudo-gang. To get into it,

You had to steal something from Circle K for more than five bucks' worth,

I remember stealing a five-pound bag of M&M's.

A couple of candy bars and a p*** magazine.
I eventually became the leader.

I had a paper route after I folded all my papers and bagged them,

And put them in my bag so that I could carry them.

And then, I would ride my bike to my routes.

On the way there, I would stop at Circle K,

Where the girl would be in the bathroom masturbating to one of the magazines,

I would steal so much s*** at that time.

I'm not proud, but that was forty years ago.

I got fired from that job because,

I wasn't very good at collecting what people owed.

I used to mow lawns, wash cars,

Anything that I could make a couple of bucks.

I would often buy my own clothes and shoes,

Remember, I was less than eleven years old at this time.

I often bought stuff for other kids.

In sixth grade, and what I thought was the hottest at the time, girls in the whole school were going steady.

I had no idea what that meant.

I played sports during break time at school.

We kissed a few times.

I remember at the end of the school day, we were in the place where the bikes were stored.

And I kissed her.

I slipt a little tongue, and she hit me in the face with her backpack. It was still worth it.

Now let me backtrack,

Just a little bit a couple of days before, as a Bible study during a break, my cousin,

Was super-hot...

I am in love with a cousin who taught me how to kiss in French.

One of the most amazing things I've ever felt in my life.

So that's why I tried it with my girlfriend in 6th grade and ended up with a black eye.

It ends up that every girl after my cousin is compared to her.

I know this now.

I didn't know this, then I probably didn't find out till I was about thirty or so.

I remember when we were still living with my uncle and my cousins.

My author uncle is only a couple of years older than me.

I performed breast surgery on my cousin with a marker.

During that time, I performed oral surgery on her.

Everybody seemed okay, and the parents never caught us; if they did, they never stopped us.

If you haven't figured it out yet since it started at such a young age,

It never seemed too bad except for the physical abuse, which always hurt,

But it always felt like it was normal.

Lying, I figured out early on, so,

I began to ignore much of what my mother and father had to say.

Jehovah's Witnesses were very good at passive indoctrination.

They would make me responsible for the turntable during meetings.

And give me readings that were supposed to make me feel big.

It worked for a while, but I began to question, for example, how they got all those animals onto the ark.

Where did they store all the food?

Where did they store all the water?

What happened to all the piss and poop?

I have gotten so much trouble for asking those questions.

I got beat,

I got starved,

I was told that all those questions would lead to my death.

As it goes to this right now, it seems like child abuse.

As you probably can tell,

I'm not a fan of Jehovah's Witnesses.

When I was about eleven years old,

I don't remember who I told,

But I told someone about my uncle abusing me.

I remember a meeting at the Kingdom Hall with two elders from Lancaster, one elder from Mojave and two elders from Bakersfield,

It was pretty much useless.

They all told me it was my fault,

I seduced my uncle,

And that if I ever spoke to anyone else outside of the congregation,

It would affect my family.

They wouldn't make it into Paradise after Armageddon.

A study was done on religious children.

What it found out,

Was that religious children don't know the difference between reality and fantasy?

Even though I was questioning things,

I still had a modicum of belief, so you can imagine the fear that those threats created,

It has been more than a decade since I was able to speak to anyone about abuse therapy, starting at about twenty-six years old.

I remember still being in junior high, hiding a bottle of Mad Dog 2020.

I had stolen from Circle K,

In a tree trunk at the back of my junior high school.

I made an excuse to go back to junior high school when an extracurricular sport was going on,

I drank that bottle,

And don't remember the rest of that night, once again,

I'm surprised I'm not dead yet.

I remember a big swimming pool part of the high school grounds, during the summer,

We would pay $0.50, and we could swim all day. It would be so much fun!

I remember jumping on a diving board several times so I would get a jump as high as I could.

I can even smell the bleach right now.

I remember hanging out outside,

On a concrete area with the sun drying us,

After we've been swimming all day, man.

So much fun!

When I was about thirteen.

Maybe fourteen. I got my first non-family girlfriend.

I had to keep her a secret from my mother.

A lot of heavy petting,

There was a lot of French kissing for hours, but no sex, though, not yet.

A girlfriend in her family went on a vacation to Cancun when they returned.

My girlfriend bought me a medallion in turquoise and silver, which is beautiful.

Somehow, even though I kept that medallion's secret as I could.

My mother found it and stole it from me.

I was so pissed.

I kicked the coffee table onto her.

Let me put it here: I've run away quite a few times at this point, about thirteen, twelve, or thirteen times.

Mojave, Bakersfield, as far as I could get, it was always brought back.

To this day, how they always found me still amazes me.

Needless to say,

The theft of my necklace led to my final runaway.

It was about ten or fifteen minutes from my girlfriend's house in the Tehachapi mountains.

I didn't know it until I got to her house.

They were pretty well off.

Her parents graciously let me stay at their house.

I don't know how, but my uncle discovered I was there.

They hid me while he came to the front door. He left.

I was there for a couple of weeks before my dad showed up.

That same day, my girlfriend's brother returned from a world trip.

This is in the early '80s. The pot is generally not so bad at this time.

He bought pot from every country he visited.

Then he mixed it all together.

He has invited me to smoke some with his friend at a barn.

Holy s***, I couldn't even walk after that.

I crawled back to the house.

They just strawberries on the way, wild.

I managed to get into the first-floor game room,

But had a very difficult time climbing several levels of stairs, when I finally got to the living room area,

There was a couch with no back there that I flopped on.

I was so stoned I fell off the couch.

I heard my girlfriend's brother talking about a supplement that helped people who got too high.

Of course, ...

later on, I learned he was messing with me,

But I reached the kitchen and found a bottle of 500 mg of niacin sitting on the marble.

I took two, and my dad showed up.

I went with him to get a hamburger in downtown Tehachapi.

We talked; this is where the first of his overt lies came into play.

I told him I didn't want to live with my mom anymore.

He said okay.

Move in with him.

I asked him if I could play sports.

He promised me, yes, that I could play sports.

When I moved in with them,

He even made an effort by taking me to buy school colors and sports equipment,

Here's the big lie.

When it came time for me to play football,

He said no.

He didn't want me mingling with the world.

It was the beginning of the end for me.

Remember, there's not a lot of help at this time for kids of abused, sexual, physical, or mental.

I remember taking the path of my family.

My thoughts were dark.

My actions were dark.

All in all, I was headed in the wrong direction.

Something clicked in my head somewhere along the line, and I chose not to be like them.

Do not ask me why it just happened.

Maybe it has to do with my ability to question Christianity and religion as a whole.

I am guessing that was about fifteen years old.

Let's go back to junior high.

My family was bent on creating a loser.

I would get good at something.

Clarinet, gymnastics, anything, like I said earlier grades,

They would take me out of those things and tell me not to be so good,

I'm not lying.

I didn't really finish anything for decades.

I started therapy, like I said, around twenty-six.

That's where we, for the first time, saw the pattern of crushing my soul,

When I was a kid, my parents used it as a tool for raising children.

My biggest achievement in forty years was returning to college as an undergrad and post-grad.

I would like to add an addendum here about therapy.

I was in therapy for several years.

It helped deal with my anger, but not all of it.

My hate for my mother. My uncle's religion grew through the decades.

Does this day I have I loathe religion?

My mother and father are dead.

I have yet to add another agendum

I wrote this little book to let other people know.

That is okay to talk about this.

It's not good to keep it to yourself.

It causes actual physical damage.

You can become very sick holding it in.

It can be very, very, very... relieving to share it with somebody with a professional.

But yet to know that you are not alone, but people care.

This sexual abuse affected me my whole life.

I never got married, I never had children, and really... really... really, caused me damage.

I know I'm not alone.

And I want to tell you. I love you...

www.ingramcontent.com/pod-product-compliance
Lightning Source LLC
LaVergne TN
LVHW051034070526
838201LV00009B/197